THE

Abundance

PLANNER

CREATED BY KAREN STOTT

#abundanceplanner
www.AnIntentionalHome.com

This planner belongs to:

_____

IF FOUND, PLEASE CONTACT ME VIA

_____

THE ABUNDANCE PLANNER IS A PRODUCT OF

Intentional Home
BY KAREN STOTT

TO CONNECT WITH KAREN VISIT
www.AnIntentionalHome.com
IG @KarenStott

If you are not yet a Young Living Member, and you want to get started,
visit www.healthyintentionalhome.com
My sponsor # is 11426948 / Haven Hill Ministries
& I'd LOVE to have you join me in this journey!

We LOVE seeing how people are using The Abundance Planner
Please use the hashtag #abundanceplanner when sharing
on social media. We will randomly choose winners from the
hashtag to win FREE goodies from our shop!

Hey Lovely!

I am seriously so honored and excited that The Abundance Planner has made its way into your hands.

This planner is a passion project for the essential oils community that I've come to know and love so much. As a busy mamapreneur, I know the struggle of the juggle well. I have been blessed to build several successful businesses over the years, grow a world-wide community of business women called Pursuit Community. And most recently, venture into the world of becoming a published author.

With everything I've had the pleasure of doing over the years, the essential oils and network marketing world is unlike anything I've ever experienced before. And I LOVE IT!

As I set out to conquer my big dreams for this business, I noticed that I was starting to hoard quite the large paper collection. Before long, I had lists, scratch notes, flow charts, and spreadsheets taking over my kitchen table. It became very clear that for me to be able to tackle my to do list, keep track of my teams growth, love my team well, plan the month ahead, and manage it all while keeping my family at the forefront, I needed a better system. I needed a hub for all of this paper mess I'd made for myself.

Within a few hours, the first Abundance Planner was underway, and I must admit, I'm a bit smitten. We all have different reasons that we started this journey, but I think we can all agree that a living a life of abundant joy, freedom, health, love, friendships, and family time is at the forefront.

I wanted to create a central place that not only allowed us to do this business well, but to do it with purpose. I want to help women work this business in a way that allows us all to thrive at life. Not just work. I hope this planner helps you to hone in on the things you do well, and delegate the rest. I hope it helps you make time for what matters, and create the business and life you've dreamed of. Because that's the good stuff friends. And it's worth fighting for.

xoxo,
Karen

Things to work on

BOOKS TO READ	VIDEOS TO MAKE	NOTES TO WRITE
_____	_____	_____
_____	_____	_____
_____	_____	_____
_____	_____	_____
_____	_____	_____
_____	_____	_____
_____	_____	_____
_____	_____	_____
_____	_____	_____
_____	_____	_____
_____	_____	_____
_____	_____	_____
_____	_____	_____
_____	_____	_____
_____	_____	_____

Dream it. See it. Do it.

WHY DID I START THIS BUSINESS?

_____

_____

_____

MY DREAM PAYCHECK

_____

MY DREAM RANK

_____

WHAT WILL BE POSSIBLE FOR ME AND MY FAMILY IF I ACHEIVE THIS RANK & PAYCHECK?

_____

_____

WHAT COULD WE DO FOR OTHERS WITH THIS RANK & PAYCHECK?

_____

_____

Gratitude List

GOOD THINGS THAT HAVE HAPPENED

_____   _____

_____   _____

_____   _____

_____   _____

_____   _____

_____   _____

_____   _____

_____   _____

_____   _____

_____   _____

_____   _____

_____   _____

_____   _____

_____   _____

Gratitude List

GOOD THINGS THAT HAVE HAPPENED

_____   _____

_____   _____

_____   _____

_____   _____

_____   _____

_____   _____

_____   _____

_____   _____

_____   _____

_____   _____

_____   _____

_____   _____

_____   _____

_____   _____

My Wheelhouse

TOP 5 STRENGTH FINDERS

_____

_____

_____

_____

_____

MEYERS - BRIGGS

_____

ENNEAGRAM

_____

MY COLORS

_____

Things to keep on my To Do's

BASED ON MY STRENGTHS & GIFTS

_____   _____

_____   _____

_____   _____

_____   _____

_____   _____

_____   _____

Not in my Wheelhouse

THINGS I DO NOT DO WELL	WHO CAN I ASK FOR HELP
_____	_____
_____	_____
_____	_____
_____	_____
_____	_____
_____	_____
_____	_____
_____	_____
_____	_____
_____	_____
_____	_____
_____	_____
_____	_____

My Systems

NEW MEMBER

_____

_____

_____

_____

_____

_____

NEW CUSTOMER

_____

_____

_____

_____

_____

_____

NEW BUILDER

_____

_____

_____

_____

_____

NEW RANKER

_____

_____

_____

_____

_____

All about Relationships

WHO TO REACH OUT TO

WHO TO FOLLOW UP WITH

_____

_____

_____

_____

_____

_____

_____

_____

_____

_____

_____

_____

_____

_____

_____

_____

_____

_____

_____

_____

_____

_____

_____

_____

_____

_____

_____

_____

Keep The Faith

WHAT TO PRAY FOR	PRAISES & ANSWERS
_____	_____
_____	_____
_____	_____
_____	_____
_____	_____
_____	_____
_____	_____
_____	_____
_____	_____
_____	_____
_____	_____
_____	_____
_____	_____
_____	_____
_____	_____

My Vision

MY VISION FOR MYSELF AND MY HEALTH IS

_____

_____

_____

MY VISION FOR MY FAMILY IS

_____

_____

_____

MY VISION FOR MY WORK IS

_____

_____

_____

MY VISION FOR MY TEAM IS

_____

_____

_____

Monthly Hub

PREVIOUS MONTH	TOTAL MEMBERS
RANK / DAY	NEW MEMBERS
OGV	PV
LEG #1 OGV	LEG #2 OGV
LEG #3 OGV	LEG #4 OGV
LEG #5 OGV	LEG #6 OGV
WHAT WENT WELL	WHAT DIDN'T

Incentives

WHO WON AN INCENTIVE	WHAT TO SEND

Monthly Hub

THIS MONTH	GOAL
_____	_____
ER INCENTIVE	BUILDER INCENTIVE
_____	_____
OGV GOAL	RANK GOAL
_____	_____
LEG #1 GOAL	LEG #2 GOAL
_____	_____
LEG #3 GOAL	LEG #4 GOAL
_____	_____
LEG #5 GOAL	LEG #6 GOAL
_____	_____
CLASSES TO HOST	PRAY FOR
_____	_____
_____	_____
_____	_____

All the Goodies

WHAT TO ADD TO ER

_____

_____

_____

_____

_____

_____

_____

_____

_____

_____

WISH LIST

_____

_____

_____

_____

_____

_____

_____

_____

_____

_____

ORDER FOR GIFTS

_____

_____

_____

_____

ORDER FOR SAMPLES

_____

_____

_____

_____

Classes

CLASS DATE

WHERE IT'S HOSTED

_____

_____

BULLET POINTS

SUPPLIES TO BUY

_____

_____

_____

_____

_____

_____

CLASS DATE

WHERE IT'S HOSTED

_____

_____

BULLET POINTS

SUPPLIES TO BUY

_____

_____

_____

_____

_____

_____

Classes

CLASS DATE

WHERE IT'S HOSTED

_____

_____

BULLET POINTS

SUPPLIES TO BUY

_____

_____

_____

_____

_____

_____

CLASS DATE

WHERE IT'S HOSTED

_____

_____

BULLET POINTS

SUPPLIES TO BUY

_____

_____

_____

_____

_____

_____

New Ranks

MEMBER NAME	RANK GIFT TO SEND
_____	_____
_____	_____
_____	_____
_____	_____
_____	_____
_____	_____
_____	_____
_____	_____
_____	_____
_____	_____
_____	_____
_____	_____
_____	_____
_____	_____

New Members

MEMBER NAME	WELCOME GIFT TO SEND
_____	_____
_____	_____
_____	_____
_____	_____
_____	_____
_____	_____
_____	_____
_____	_____
_____	_____
_____	_____
_____	_____
_____	_____
_____	_____
_____	_____

Goal Hub

MY CURRENT	MY GOAL
LEG #1 CURRENT	THEIR GOAL
LEG #2 CURRENT	THEIR GOAL
LEG #3 CURRENT	THEIR GOAL
LEG #4 CURRENT	THEIR GOAL
LEG #5 CURRENT	THEIR GOAL
LEG #6 CURRENT	THEIR GOAL

My Rank Map

FRONTLINE TEAM

Leg #1

NAME

BIRTHDAY

_____

_____

GOALS

FAVORITE PRODUCTS

_____

_____

Rank Map

Leg #2

NAME

BIRTHDAY

_____

_____

GOALS

FAVORITE PRODUCTS

_____

_____

Rank Map

Leg #3

NAME

BIRTHDAY

_____

_____

GOALS

FAVORITE PRODUCTS

_____

_____

Rank Map

Leg #4

NAME

BIRTHDAY

GOALS

FAVORITE PRODUCTS

Rank Map

Leg #5

NAME

BIRTHDAY

_____

_____

GOALS

FAVORITE PRODUCTS

_____

_____

Rank Map

Leg #6

NAME

BIRTHDAY

_____

_____

GOALS

FAVORITE PRODUCTS

_____

_____

Rank Map

IT'S _____   SUNDAY   MONDAY   TUESDAY

THANKFUL FOR

_____
_____
_____
_____
_____
_____
_____
_____
_____
_____
_____
_____
_____
_____
_____
_____
_____
_____

WEDNESDAY	THURSDAY	FRIDAY	SATURDAY

Week of ____________________

TO DO'S	NOTES		MONDAY	TUESDAY
for life		TOP 3 TO DO'S		
for work		THINGS TO DO NEXT		
		TODAY'S GOOD THINGS		

WEDNESDAY	THURSDAY	FRIDAY	SAT & SUN

Week of _____

TO DO'S	NOTES		MONDAY	TUESDAY
for life	_____	**TOP 3 TO DO'S**		
_____	_____			
_____	_____			
_____	_____			
_____	_____			
_____	_____	**THINGS TO DO NEXT**		
_____	_____			
_____	_____			
for work	_____			
_____	_____			
_____	_____			
_____	_____			
_____	_____			
_____	_____	**TODAY'S GOOD THINGS**		
_____	_____			
_____	_____			

WEDNESDAY	THURSDAY	FRIDAY	SAT & SUN

Week of _____

TO DO'S	NOTES		MONDAY	TUESDAY
for life		**TOP 3 TO DO'S**		
for work		**THINGS TO DO NEXT**		
		TODAY'S GOOD THINGS		

WEDNESDAY	THURSDAY	FRIDAY	SAT & SUN

Week of _____

TO DO'S	NOTES		MONDAY	TUESDAY
for life	_____	**TOP 3 TO DO'S**		
_____	_____			
_____	_____			
_____	_____			
_____	_____			
_____	_____	**THINGS TO DO NEXT**		
_____	_____			
for work	_____			
_____	_____			
_____	_____			
_____	_____			
_____	_____	**TODAY'S GOOD THINGS**		
_____	_____			
_____	_____			

WEDNESDAY	THURSDAY	FRIDAY	SAT & SUN

Week of _____

TO DO'S	NOTES		MONDAY	TUESDAY
for life	_____	**TOP 3 TO DO'S**		
_____	_____			
_____	_____			
_____	_____			
_____	_____			
_____	_____	**THINGS TO DO NEXT**		
_____	_____			
_____	_____			
for work	_____			
_____	_____			
_____	_____			
_____	_____			
_____	_____	**TODAY'S GOOD THINGS**		
_____	_____			
_____	_____			
_____	_____			

WEDNESDAY	THURSDAY	FRIDAY	SAT & SUN

Monthly Hub

PREVIOUS MONTH	TOTAL MEMBERS
RANK / DAY	NEW MEMBERS
OGV	PV
LEG #1 OGV	LEG #2 OGV
LEG #3 OGV	LEG #4 OGV
LEG #5 OGV	LEG #6 OGV
WHAT WENT WELL	WHAT DIDN'T

Incentives

WHO WON AN INCENTIVE	WHAT TO SEND

Monthly Hub

THIS MONTH	GOAL
_____	_____
ER INCENTIVE	BUILDER INCENTIVE
_____	_____
OGV GOAL	RANK GOAL
_____	_____
LEG #1 GOAL	LEG #2 GOAL
_____	_____
LEG #3 GOAL	LEG #4 GOAL
_____	_____
LEG #5 GOAL	LEG #6 GOAL
_____	_____
CLASSES TO HOST	PRAY FOR
_____	_____
_____	_____
_____	_____

All the Goodies

WHAT TO ADD TO ER

_____

_____

_____

_____

_____

_____

_____

_____

_____

_____

ORDER FOR GIFTS

_____

_____

_____

_____

WISH LIST

_____

_____

_____

_____

_____

_____

_____

_____

_____

_____

ORDER FOR SAMPLES

_____

_____

_____

_____

Classes

CLASS DATE

WHERE IT'S HOSTED

_____

_____

BULLET POINTS

SUPPLIES TO BUY

_____

_____

_____

_____

_____

_____

CLASS DATE

WHERE IT'S HOSTED

_____

_____

BULLET POINTS

SUPPLIES TO BUY

_____

_____

_____

_____

_____

_____

Classes

CLASS DATE

WHERE IT'S HOSTED

_____

_____

BULLET POINTS

SUPPLIES TO BUY

_____

_____

_____

_____

_____

_____

CLASS DATE

WHERE IT'S HOSTED

_____

_____

BULLET POINTS

SUPPLIES TO BUY

_____

_____

_____

_____

_____

_____

New Ranks

MEMBER NAME	RANK GIFT TO SEND

New Members

MEMBER NAME	WELCOME GIFT TO SEND

Goal Hub

MY CURRENT	MY GOAL
LEG #1 CURRENT	THEIR GOAL
LEG #2 CURRENT	THEIR GOAL
LEG #3 CURRENT	THEIR GOAL
LEG #4 CURRENT	THEIR GOAL
LEG #5 CURRENT	THEIR GOAL
LEG #6 CURRENT	THEIR GOAL

My Rank Map

FRONTLINE TEAM

Leg #1

NAME

BIRTHDAY

_____

_____

GOALS

FAVORITE PRODUCTS

_____

_____

Rank Map

leg #2

NAME

BIRTHDAY

GOALS

FAVORITE PRODUCTS

Rank Map

Leg #3

NAME   BIRTHDAY

_____   _____

GOALS   FAVORITE PRODUCTS

_____   _____

Rank Map

Leg #4

NAME

BIRTHDAY

_____

_____

GOALS

FAVORITE PRODUCTS

_____

_____

Rank Map

Leg #5

NAME	BIRTHDAY

GOALS	FAVORITE PRODUCTS

Rank Map

Leg #6

NAME

BIRTHDAY

_____

_____

GOALS

FAVORITE PRODUCTS

_____

_____

Rank Map

IT'S _____   SUNDAY   MONDAY   TUESDAY

THANKFUL FOR

_____
_____
_____
_____
_____
_____
_____
_____
_____
_____
_____
_____
_____
_____
_____
_____
_____
_____
_____

WEDNESDAY	THURSDAY	FRIDAY	SATURDAY

Week of _____

TO DO'S	NOTES		MONDAY	TUESDAY

for life

_____

_____

_____

_____

_____

_____

_____

_____

for work

_____

_____

_____

_____

_____

_____

_____

_____

TOP 3 TO DO'S

THINGS TO DO NEXT

TODAY'S GOOD THINGS

WEDNESDAY	THURSDAY	FRIDAY	SAT & SUN

Week of _____

TO DO'S	NOTES		MONDAY	TUESDAY
for life	_____	TOP 3 TO DO'S		
_____	_____			
_____	_____			
_____	_____			
_____	_____	THINGS TO DO NEXT		
_____	_____			
_____	_____			
for work	_____			
_____	_____			
_____	_____			
_____	_____			
_____	_____	TODAY'S GOOD THINGS		
_____	_____			
_____	_____			

WEDNESDAY	THURSDAY	FRIDAY	SAT & SUN

Week of _____

TO DO'S	NOTES		MONDAY	TUESDAY
for life	_____	**TOP 3 TO DO'S**		
_____	_____			
_____	_____			
_____	_____			
_____	_____			
_____	_____			
_____	_____	**THINGS TO DO NEXT**		
_____	_____			
for work	_____			
_____	_____			
_____	_____			
_____	_____			
_____	_____	**TODAY'S GOOD THINGS**		
_____	_____			
_____	_____			

WEDNESDAY	THURSDAY	FRIDAY	SAT & SUN

Week of _____

TO DO'S	NOTES		MONDAY	TUESDAY
for life	_____	**TOP 3 TO DO'S**		
_____	_____			
_____	_____			
_____	_____			
_____	_____			
_____	_____	**THINGS TO DO NEXT**		
_____	_____			
_____	_____			
for work	_____			
_____	_____			
_____	_____			
_____	_____			
_____	_____	**TODAY'S GOOD THINGS**		
_____	_____			
_____	_____			

WEDNESDAY	THURSDAY	FRIDAY	SAT & SUN

Week of _____

TO DO'S	NOTES		MONDAY	TUESDAY
for life	_____	**TOP 3 TO DO'S**		
_____	_____			
_____	_____			
_____	_____			
_____	_____			
_____	_____	**THINGS TO DO NEXT**		
_____	_____			
_____	_____			
for work	_____			
_____	_____			
_____	_____			
_____	_____			
_____	_____	**TODAY'S GOOD THINGS**		
_____	_____			
_____	_____			

WEDNESDAY	THURSDAY	FRIDAY	SAT & SUN

Monthly Hub

PREVIOUS MONTH	TOTAL MEMBERS
RANK / DAY	NEW MEMBERS
OGV	PV
LEG #1 OGV	LEG #2 OGV
LEG #3 OGV	LEG #4 OGV
LEG #5 OGV	LEG #6 OGV
WHAT WENT WELL	WHAT DIDN'T

Incentives

WHO WON AN INCENTIVE	WHAT TO SEND

Monthly Hub

THIS MONTH	GOAL
ER INCENTIVE	BUILDER INCENTIVE
OGV GOAL	RANK GOAL
LEG #1 GOAL	LEG #2 GOAL
LEG #3 GOAL	LEG #4 GOAL
LEG #5 GOAL	LEG #6 GOAL
CLASSES TO HOST	PRAY FOR

All the Goodies

WHAT TO ADD TO ER

_____

_____

_____

_____

_____

_____

_____

_____

_____

WISH LIST

_____

_____

_____

_____

_____

_____

_____

_____

_____

ORDER FOR GIFTS

_____

_____

_____

_____

ORDER FOR SAMPLES

_____

_____

_____

_____

Classes

CLASS DATE

_____

WHERE IT'S HOSTED

_____

BULLET POINTS

_____

_____

_____

SUPPLIES TO BUY

_____

_____

_____

CLASS DATE

_____

WHERE IT'S HOSTED

_____

BULLET POINTS

_____

_____

_____

SUPPLIES TO BUY

_____

_____

_____

Classes

CLASS DATE

WHERE IT'S HOSTED

_____

_____

BULLET POINTS

SUPPLIES TO BUY

_____

_____

_____

_____

_____

_____

CLASS DATE

WHERE IT'S HOSTED

_____

_____

BULLET POINTS

SUPPLIES TO BUY

_____

_____

_____

_____

_____

_____

New Ranks

MEMBER NAME	RANK GIFT TO SEND
_____	_____
_____	_____
_____	_____
_____	_____
_____	_____
_____	_____
_____	_____
_____	_____
_____	_____
_____	_____
_____	_____
_____	_____
_____	_____
_____	_____

New Members

MEMBER NAME	WELCOME GIFT TO SEND

Goal Hub

MY CURRENT	MY GOAL
LEG #1 CURRENT	THEIR GOAL
LEG #2 CURRENT	THEIR GOAL
LEG #3 CURRENT	THEIR GOAL
LEG #4 CURRENT	THEIR GOAL
LEG #5 CURRENT	THEIR GOAL
LEG #6 CURRENT	THEIR GOAL

My Rank Map

FRONTLINE TEAM

Leg #1

NAME   BIRTHDAY

_____   _____

GOALS   FAVORITE PRODUCTS

_____   _____

Rank Map

Leg #2

NAME

BIRTHDAY

GOALS

FAVORITE PRODUCTS

Rank Map

Leg #3

NAME   BIRTHDAY

GOALS   FAVORITE PRODUCTS

Rank Map

Leg #4

NAME

BIRTHDAY

GOALS

FAVORITE PRODUCTS

Rank Map

leg #5

NAME

BIRTHDAY

_____

_____

GOALS

FAVORITE PRODUCTS

_____

_____

Rank Map

Leg #6

NAME

BIRTHDAY

_____

_____

GOALS

FAVORITE PRODUCTS

_____

_____

Rank Map

IT'S _____ SUNDAY MONDAY TUESDAY

THANKFUL FOR

_____
_____
_____
_____
_____
_____
_____
_____
_____
_____
_____
_____
_____
_____
_____
_____
_____
_____

WEDNESDAY	THURSDAY	FRIDAY	SATURDAY

Week of _____

TO DO'S	NOTES		MONDAY	TUESDAY
for life	_____	**TOP 3 TO DO'S**		
_____	_____			
_____	_____			
_____	_____			
_____	_____			
_____	_____			
_____	_____			
_____	_____	**THINGS TO DO NEXT**		
for work	_____			
_____	_____			
_____	_____			
_____	_____			
_____	_____	**TODAY'S GOOD THINGS**		
_____	_____			
_____	_____			

WEDNESDAY	THURSDAY	FRIDAY	SAT & SUN

Week of _____

TO DO'S	NOTES		MONDAY	TUESDAY
for life		**TOP 3 TO DO'S**		
		THINGS TO DO NEXT		
for work				
		TODAY'S GOOD THINGS		

WEDNESDAY	THURSDAY	FRIDAY	SAT & SUN

Week of _____

TO DO'S	NOTES		MONDAY	TUESDAY
for life	_____	**TOP 3 TO DO'S**		
_____	_____			
_____	_____			
_____	_____			
_____	_____			
_____	_____	**THINGS TO DO NEXT**		
_____	_____			
_____	_____			
for work	_____			
_____	_____			
_____	_____			
_____	_____			
_____	_____	**TODAY'S GOOD THINGS**		
_____	_____			
_____	_____			
_____	_____			

WEDNESDAY	THURSDAY	FRIDAY	SAT & SUN

Week of _____

TO DO'S	NOTES		MONDAY	TUESDAY
for life	_____	**TOP 3 TO DO'S**		
_____	_____			
_____	_____			
_____	_____			
_____	_____			
_____	_____			
_____	_____	**THINGS TO DO NEXT**		
_____	_____			
_____	_____			
for work	_____			
_____	_____			
_____	_____			
_____	_____			
_____	_____	**TODAY'S GOOD THINGS**		
_____	_____			
_____	_____			
_____	_____			

WEDNESDAY	THURSDAY	FRIDAY	SAT & SUN

Week of _____

TO DO'S	NOTES		MONDAY	TUESDAY
for life	_____	TOP 3 TO DO'S		
_____	_____			
_____	_____			
_____	_____			
_____	_____	THINGS TO DO NEXT		
_____	_____			
_____	_____			
for work	_____			
_____	_____			
_____	_____			
_____	_____			
_____	_____	TODAY'S GOOD THINGS		
_____	_____			
_____	_____			

WEDNESDAY	THURSDAY	FRIDAY	SAT & SUN

Monthly Hub

PREVIOUS MONTH	TOTAL MEMBERS
RANK / DAY	NEW MEMBERS
OGV	PV
LEG #1 OGV	LEG #2 OGV
LEG #3 OGV	LEG #4 OGV
LEG #5 OGV	LEG #6 OGV
WHAT WENT WELL	WHAT DIDN'T

Incentives

WHO WON AN INCENTIVE	WHAT TO SEND

Monthly Hub

THIS MONTH	GOAL
ER INCENTIVE	BUILDER INCENTIVE
OGV GOAL	RANK GOAL
LEG #1 GOAL	LEG #2 GOAL
LEG #3 GOAL	LEG #4 GOAL
LEG #5 GOAL	LEG #6 GOAL
CLASSES TO HOST	PRAY FOR

All the Goodies

WHAT TO ADD TO ER   WISH LIST

_____   _____

_____   _____

_____   _____

_____   _____

_____   _____

_____   _____

_____   _____

_____   _____

_____   _____

_____   _____

ORDER FOR GIFTS   ORDER FOR SAMPLES

_____   _____

_____   _____

_____   _____

_____   _____

Classes

CLASS DATE

WHERE IT'S HOSTED

_____

_____

BULLET POINTS

SUPPLIES TO BUY

_____

_____

_____

_____

_____

_____

CLASS DATE

WHERE IT'S HOSTED

_____

_____

BULLET POINTS

SUPPLIES TO BUY

_____

_____

_____

_____

_____

_____

Classes

CLASS DATE

WHERE IT'S HOSTED

_____

_____

BULLET POINTS

SUPPLIES TO BUY

_____

_____

_____

_____

_____

_____

CLASS DATE

WHERE IT'S HOSTED

_____

_____

BULLET POINTS

SUPPLIES TO BUY

_____

_____

_____

_____

_____

_____

New Ranks

MEMBER NAME	RANK GIFT TO SEND

New Members

MEMBER NAME	WELCOME GIFT TO SEND

Goal Hub

MY CURRENT	MY GOAL
LEG #1 CURRENT	THEIR GOAL
LEG #2 CURRENT	THEIR GOAL
LEG #3 CURRENT	THEIR GOAL
LEG #4 CURRENT	THEIR GOAL
LEG #5 CURRENT	THEIR GOAL
LEG #6 CURRENT	THEIR GOAL

My Rank Map

FRONTLINE TEAM

Leg #1

NAME   BIRTHDAY

_____   _____

GOALS   FAVORITE PRODUCTS

_____   _____

Rank Map

Leg #2

NAME

BIRTHDAY

_____

_____

GOALS

FAVORITE PRODUCTS

_____

_____

Rank Map

Leg #3

NAME

BIRTHDAY

_____

_____

GOALS

FAVORITE PRODUCTS

_____

_____

Rank Map

Leg #4

NAME

BIRTHDAY

GOALS

FAVORITE PRODUCTS

Rank Map

Leg #5

NAME

BIRTHDAY

_____

_____

GOALS

FAVORITE PRODUCTS

_____

_____

Rank Map

Leg #6

NAME   BIRTHDAY

GOALS   FAVORITE PRODUCTS

Rank Map

IT'S _____   SUNDAY   MONDAY   TUESDAY

THANKFUL FOR

_____

_____

_____

_____

_____

_____

_____

_____

_____

_____

_____

_____

_____

_____

_____

_____

_____

_____

WEDNESDAY	THURSDAY	FRIDAY	SATURDAY

Week of _____

TO DO'S	NOTES		MONDAY	TUESDAY
for life	_____	**TOP 3 TO DO'S**		
		THINGS TO DO NEXT		
for work				
		TODAY'S GOOD THINGS		

WEDNESDAY	THURSDAY	FRIDAY	SAT & SUN

Week of _____

TO DO'S	NOTES		MONDAY	TUESDAY
for life	_____	TOP 3 TO DO'S		
_____	_____			
_____	_____			
_____	_____			
_____	_____			
_____	_____			
_____	_____	THINGS TO DO NEXT		
_____	_____			
for work	_____			
_____	_____			
_____	_____			
_____	_____			
_____	_____	TODAY'S GOOD THINGS		
_____	_____			
_____	_____			

WEDNESDAY	THURSDAY	FRIDAY	SAT & SUN

Week of _____

TO DO'S	NOTES		MONDAY	TUESDAY
for life		TOP 3 TO DO'S		
for work		THINGS TO DO NEXT		
		TODAY'S GOOD THINGS		

WEDNESDAY	THURSDAY	FRIDAY	SAT & SUN

Week of _____

	TO DO'S	NOTES		MONDAY	TUESDAY

TO DO'S

for life

for work

NOTES

TOP 3 TO DO'S

THINGS TO DO NEXT

TODAY'S GOOD THINGS

MONDAY

TUESDAY

WEDNESDAY	THURSDAY	FRIDAY	SAT & SUN

Week of _____

TO DO'S	NOTES		MONDAY	TUESDAY
for life	_____	**TOP 3 TO DO'S**		
_____	_____			
_____	_____			
_____	_____			
_____	_____			
_____	_____			
_____	_____	**THINGS TO DO NEXT**		
_____	_____			
_____	_____			
for work	_____			
_____	_____			
_____	_____			
_____	_____			
_____	_____			
_____	_____	**TODAY'S GOOD THINGS**		
_____	_____			
_____	_____			

WEDNESDAY	THURSDAY	FRIDAY	SAT & SUN

Monthly Hub

PREVIOUS MONTH	TOTAL MEMBERS
_____	_____
RANK / DAY	NEW MEMBERS
_____	_____
OGV	PV
_____	_____
LEG #1 OGV	LEG #2 OGV
_____	_____
LEG #3 OGV	LEG #4 OGV
_____	_____
LEG #5 OGV	LEG #6 OGV
_____	_____
WHAT WENT WELL	WHAT DIDN'T
_____	_____
_____	_____
_____	_____

Incentives

WHO WON AN INCENTIVE	WHAT TO SEND

Monthly Hub

THIS MONTH	GOAL
ER INCENTIVE	BUILDER INCENTIVE
OGV GOAL	RANK GOAL
LEG #1 GOAL	LEG #2 GOAL
LEG #3 GOAL	LEG #4 GOAL
LEG #5 GOAL	LEG #6 GOAL
CLASSES TO HOST	PRAY FOR

All the Goodies

WHAT TO ADD TO ER

_____

_____

_____

_____

_____

_____

_____

_____

_____

WISH LIST

_____

_____

_____

_____

_____

_____

_____

_____

_____

ORDER FOR GIFTS

_____

_____

_____

ORDER FOR SAMPLES

_____

_____

_____

Classes

CLASS DATE	WHERE IT'S HOSTED

BULLET POINTS	SUPPLIES TO BUY

CLASS DATE	WHERE IT'S HOSTED

BULLET POINTS	SUPPLIES TO BUY

Classes

CLASS DATE

WHERE IT'S HOSTED

_____

_____

BULLET POINTS

SUPPLIES TO BUY

_____

_____

_____

_____

_____

_____

CLASS DATE

WHERE IT'S HOSTED

_____

_____

BULLET POINTS

SUPPLIES TO BUY

_____

_____

_____

_____

_____

_____

New Ranks

MEMBER NAME	RANK GIFT TO SEND
_____	_____
_____	_____
_____	_____
_____	_____
_____	_____
_____	_____
_____	_____
_____	_____
_____	_____
_____	_____
_____	_____
_____	_____
_____	_____

New Members

MEMBER NAME	WELCOME GIFT TO SEND

Goal Hub

MY CURRENT	MY GOAL
LEG #1 CURRENT	THEIR GOAL
LEG #2 CURRENT	THEIR GOAL
LEG #3 CURRENT	THEIR GOAL
LEG #4 CURRENT	THEIR GOAL
LEG #5 CURRENT	THEIR GOAL
LEG #6 CURRENT	THEIR GOAL

My Rank Map

FRONTLINE TEAM

Leg #1

NAME   BIRTHDAY

_____   _____

GOALS   FAVORITE PRODUCTS

_____   _____

Rank Map

Leg #2

NAME

BIRTHDAY

_____

_____

GOALS

FAVORITE PRODUCTS

_____

_____

Rank Map

Leg #3

NAME

BIRTHDAY

_____

_____

GOALS

FAVORITE PRODUCTS

_____

_____

Rank Map

leg #4

NAME

BIRTHDAY

GOALS

FAVORITE PRODUCTS

Rank Map

Leg #5

NAME

BIRTHDAY

_____

_____

GOALS

FAVORITE PRODUCTS

_____

_____

Rank Map

Leg #6

NAME

BIRTHDAY

_____

_____

GOALS

FAVORITE PRODUCTS

_____

_____

Rank Map

IT'S _____   SUNDAY   MONDAY   TUESDAY

THANKFUL FOR

_____

_____

_____

_____

_____

_____

_____

_____

_____

_____

_____

_____

_____

_____

_____

_____

_____

_____

_____

WEDNESDAY	THURSDAY	FRIDAY	SATURDAY

Week of _____

TO DO'S	NOTES		MONDAY	TUESDAY
for life	_____			
_____	_____			
_____	_____			
_____	_____	TOP 3 TO DO'S		
_____	_____			
_____	_____			
_____	_____			
_____	_____			
for work	_____	THINGS TO DO NEXT		
_____	_____			
_____	_____			
_____	_____			
_____	_____	TODAY'S GOOD THINGS		
_____	_____			

WEDNESDAY	THURSDAY	FRIDAY	SAT & SUN

Week of _____

TO DO'S	NOTES		MONDAY	TUESDAY
for life	_____	TOP 3 TO DO'S		
_____	_____			
_____	_____			
_____	_____			
_____	_____			
_____	_____	THINGS TO DO NEXT		
_____	_____			
_____	_____			
for work	_____			
_____	_____			
_____	_____			
_____	_____			
_____	_____	TODAY'S GOOD THINGS		
_____	_____			
_____	_____			

WEDNESDAY	THURSDAY	FRIDAY	SAT & SUN

Week of _____

TO DO'S	NOTES		MONDAY	TUESDAY
for life	_____	**TOP 3 TO DO'S**		
_____	_____			
_____	_____			
_____	_____			
_____	_____			
_____	_____	**THINGS TO DO NEXT**		
_____	_____			
_____	_____			
_____	_____			
for work	_____			
_____	_____			
_____	_____			
_____	_____			
_____	_____	**TODAY'S GOOD THINGS**		
_____	_____			
_____	_____			
_____	_____			

WEDNESDAY	THURSDAY	FRIDAY	SAT & SUN

Week of _____

TO DO'S	NOTES		MONDAY	TUESDAY

for life

_____

_____

_____

_____

_____

_____

_____

_____

_____

for work

_____

_____

_____

_____

_____

_____

_____

_____

NOTES column:
_____

_____

_____

_____

_____

_____

_____

_____

_____

_____

_____

_____

_____

_____

TOP 3 TO DO'S

THINGS TO DO NEXT

TODAY'S GOOD THINGS

WEDNESDAY	THURSDAY	FRIDAY	SAT & SUN

Week of _____

TO DO'S	NOTES		MONDAY	TUESDAY

for life

for work

TOP 3 TO DO'S

THINGS TO DO NEXT

TODAY'S GOOD THINGS

WEDNESDAY	THURSDAY	FRIDAY	SAT & SUN

Monthly Hub

PREVIOUS MONTH	TOTAL MEMBERS
RANK / DAY	NEW MEMBERS
OGV	PV
LEG #1 OGV	LEG #2 OGV
LEG #3 OGV	LEG #4 OGV
LEG #5 OGV	LEG #6 OGV
WHAT WENT WELL	WHAT DIDN'T

Incentives

WHO WON AN INCENTIVE	WHAT TO SEND
_____	_____
_____	_____
_____	_____
_____	_____
_____	_____
_____	_____
_____	_____
_____	_____
_____	_____
_____	_____
_____	_____
_____	_____
_____	_____
_____	_____
_____	_____

Monthly Hub

THIS MONTH	GOAL
ER INCENTIVE	BUILDER INCENTIVE
OGV GOAL	RANK GOAL
LEG #1 GOAL	LEG #2 GOAL
LEG #3 GOAL	LEG #4 GOAL
LEG #5 GOAL	LEG #6 GOAL
CLASSES TO HOST	PRAY FOR

All the Goodies

WHAT TO ADD TO ER

_____

_____

_____

_____

_____

_____

_____

_____

_____

WISH LIST

_____

_____

_____

_____

_____

_____

_____

_____

_____

ORDER FOR GIFTS

_____

_____

_____

ORDER FOR SAMPLES

_____

_____

_____

Classes

CLASS DATE

_____

WHERE IT'S HOSTED

_____

BULLET POINTS

_____

_____

_____

SUPPLIES TO BUY

_____

_____

_____

CLASS DATE

_____

WHERE IT'S HOSTED

_____

BULLET POINTS

_____

_____

_____

SUPPLIES TO BUY

_____

_____

_____

Classes

CLASS DATE

WHERE IT'S HOSTED

_____

_____

BULLET POINTS

SUPPLIES TO BUY

_____

_____

_____

_____

_____

_____

CLASS DATE

WHERE IT'S HOSTED

_____

_____

BULLET POINTS

SUPPLIES TO BUY

_____

_____

_____

_____

_____

_____

New Ranks

MEMBER NAME	RANK GIFT TO SEND
_____	_____
_____	_____
_____	_____
_____	_____
_____	_____
_____	_____
_____	_____
_____	_____
_____	_____
_____	_____
_____	_____
_____	_____
_____	_____
_____	_____

New Members

MEMBER NAME	WELCOME GIFT TO SEND
_____	_____
_____	_____
_____	_____
_____	_____
_____	_____
_____	_____
_____	_____
_____	_____
_____	_____
_____	_____
_____	_____
_____	_____
_____	_____
_____	_____

Goal Hub

MY CURRENT	MY GOAL
LEG #1 CURRENT	THEIR GOAL
LEG #2 CURRENT	THEIR GOAL
LEG #3 CURRENT	THEIR GOAL
LEG #4 CURRENT	THEIR GOAL
LEG #5 CURRENT	THEIR GOAL
LEG #6 CURRENT	THEIR GOAL

My Rank Map

FRONTLINE TEAM

Leg #1

NAME

BIRTHDAY

_____

_____

GOALS

FAVORITE PRODUCTS

_____

_____

Rank Map

Leg #2

NAME

BIRTHDAY

_____

_____

GOALS

FAVORITE PRODUCTS

_____

_____

Rank Map

Leg #3

NAME

BIRTHDAY

_____

_____

GOALS

FAVORITE PRODUCTS

_____

_____

Rank Map

Leg #4

NAME

BIRTHDAY

GOALS

FAVORITE PRODUCTS

Rank Map

Leg #5

NAME

BIRTHDAY

_____

_____

GOALS

FAVORITE PRODUCTS

_____

_____

Rank Map

Leg #6

NAME

BIRTHDAY

_____

_____

GOALS

FAVORITE PRODUCTS

_____

_____

Rank Map

IT'S _____	SUNDAY	MONDAY	TUESDAY
THANKFUL FOR			
_____			
_____			
_____			
_____			
_____			
_____			
_____			
_____			
_____			
_____			
_____			
_____			
_____			
_____			
_____			
_____			
_____			
_____			
_____			
_____			

WEDNESDAY	THURSDAY	FRIDAY	SATURDAY

Week of _____

TO DO'S	NOTES		MONDAY	TUESDAY
for life	_____	**TOP 3 TO DO'S**		
_____	_____			
_____	_____			
_____	_____			
_____	_____			
_____	_____	**THINGS TO DO NEXT**		
_____	_____			
_____	_____			
for work	_____			
_____	_____			
_____	_____			
_____	_____			
_____	_____	**TODAY'S GOOD THINGS**		
_____	_____			
_____	_____			

WEDNESDAY	THURSDAY	FRIDAY	SAT & SUN

Week of _____

TO DO'S	NOTES		MONDAY	TUESDAY
for life	_____	**TOP 3 TO DO'S**		
_____	_____			
_____	_____			
_____	_____			
_____	_____			
_____	_____	**THINGS TO DO NEXT**		
_____	_____			
_____	_____			
for work	_____			
_____	_____			
_____	_____			
_____	_____			
_____	_____	**TODAY'S GOOD THINGS**		
_____	_____			
_____	_____			

WEDNESDAY	THURSDAY	FRIDAY	SAT & SUN

Week of _____

TO DO'S	NOTES		MONDAY	TUESDAY
for life	_____	TOP 3 TO DO'S		
_____	_____			
_____	_____			
_____	_____			
_____	_____			
_____	_____			
_____	_____	THINGS TO DO NEXT		
for work	_____			
_____	_____			
_____	_____			
_____	_____			
_____	_____	TODAY'S GOOD THINGS		
_____	_____			

WEDNESDAY	THURSDAY	FRIDAY	SAT & SUN

Week of _____

TO DO'S	NOTES		MONDAY	TUESDAY
for life	_____	**TOP 3 TO DO'S**		
_____	_____			
_____	_____			
_____	_____			
_____	_____			
_____	_____	**THINGS TO DO NEXT**		
_____	_____			
_____	_____			
for work	_____			
_____	_____			
_____	_____			
_____	_____			
_____	_____	**TODAY'S GOOD THINGS**		
_____	_____			
_____	_____			

WEDNESDAY	THURSDAY	FRIDAY	SAT & SUN

Week of _____

TO DO'S	NOTES		MONDAY	TUESDAY
for life	_____	**TOP 3 TO DO'S**		
_____	_____			
_____	_____			
_____	_____			
_____	_____	**THINGS TO DO NEXT**		
_____	_____			
_____	_____			
for work	_____			
_____	_____			
_____	_____			
_____	_____			
_____	_____	**TODAY'S GOOD THINGS**		
_____	_____			
_____	_____			

WEDNESDAY	THURSDAY	FRIDAY	SAT & SUN

Sample Requests

Name _____

Address _____

_____

Sample _____

Conversation Via _____

Sent _____ Follow Up _____

Enrolled _____ Stacked _____

Notes _____

_____

_____

Name _____

Address _____

_____

Sample _____

Conversation Via _____

Sent _____ Follow Up _____

Enrolled _____ Stacked _____

Notes _____

_____

_____

Name _____

Address _____

_____

Sample _____

Conversation Via _____

Sent _____ Follow Up _____

Enrolled _____ Stacked _____

Notes _____

_____

_____

Name _____

Address _____

_____

Sample _____

Conversation Via _____

Sent _____ Follow Up _____

Enrolled _____ Stacked _____

Notes _____

_____

_____

Sample Requests

Name _____

Address _____

_____

Sample _____

Conversation Via _____

Sent _____ Follow Up _____

Enrolled _____ Stacked _____

Notes _____

_____

_____

Name _____

Address _____

_____

Sample _____

Conversation Via _____

Sent _____ Follow Up _____

Enrolled _____ Stacked _____

Notes _____

_____

_____

Name _____

Address _____

_____

Sample _____

Conversation Via _____

Sent _____ Follow Up _____

Enrolled _____ Stacked _____

Notes _____

_____

_____

Name _____

Address _____

_____

Sample _____

Conversation Via _____

Sent _____ Follow Up _____

Enrolled _____ Stacked _____

Notes _____

_____

_____

Sample Requests

Name _____

Address _____

_____

Sample _____

Conversation Via _____

Sent _____ Follow Up _____

Enrolled _____ Stacked _____

Notes _____

_____

_____

Name _____

Address _____

_____

Sample _____

Conversation Via _____

Sent _____ Follow Up _____

Enrolled _____ Stacked _____

Notes _____

_____

_____

Name _____

Address _____

_____

Sample _____

Conversation Via _____

Sent _____ Follow Up _____

Enrolled _____ Stacked _____

Notes _____

_____

_____

Name _____

Address _____

_____

Sample _____

Conversation Via _____

Sent _____ Follow Up _____

Enrolled _____ Stacked _____

Notes _____

_____

_____

Sample Requests

Name _____

Address _____

_____

Sample _____

Conversation Via _____

Sent _____ Follow Up _____

Enrolled _____ Stacked _____

Notes _____

_____

_____

Name _____

Address _____

_____

Sample _____

Conversation Via _____

Sent _____ Follow Up _____

Enrolled _____ Stacked _____

Notes _____

_____

_____

Name _____

Address _____

_____

Sample _____

Conversation Via _____

Sent _____ Follow Up _____

Enrolled _____ Stacked _____

Notes _____

_____

_____

Name _____

Address _____

_____

Sample _____

Conversation Via _____

Sent _____ Follow Up _____

Enrolled _____ Stacked _____

Notes _____

_____

_____

Sample Requests

Name _____

Address _____

_____

Sample _____

Conversation Via _____

Sent _____ Follow Up _____

Enrolled _____ Stacked _____

Notes _____

_____

_____

Name _____

Address _____

_____

Sample _____

Conversation Via _____

Sent _____ Follow Up _____

Enrolled _____ Stacked _____

Notes _____

_____

_____

Name _____

Address _____

_____

Sample _____

Conversation Via _____

Sent _____ Follow Up _____

Enrolled _____ Stacked _____

Notes _____

_____

_____

Name _____

Address _____

_____

Sample _____

Conversation Via _____

Sent _____ Follow Up _____

Enrolled _____ Stacked _____

Notes _____

_____

_____

Sample Requests

Name _____

Address _____

_____

Sample _____

Conversation Via _____

Sent _____ Follow Up _____

Enrolled _____ Stacked _____

Notes _____

_____

_____

Name _____

Address _____

_____

Sample _____

Conversation Via _____

Sent _____ Follow Up _____

Enrolled _____ Stacked _____

Notes _____

_____

_____

Name _____

Address _____

_____

Sample _____

Conversation Via _____

Sent _____ Follow Up _____

Enrolled _____ Stacked _____

Notes _____

_____

_____

Name _____

Address _____

_____

Sample _____

Conversation Via _____

Sent _____ Follow Up _____

Enrolled _____ Stacked _____

Notes _____

_____

_____

Sample Requests

Name _____

Address _____

_____

Sample _____

Conversation Via _____

Sent _____ Follow Up _____

Enrolled _____ Stacked _____

Notes _____

_____

_____

Name _____

Address _____

_____

Sample _____

Conversation Via _____

Sent _____ Follow Up _____

Enrolled _____ Stacked _____

Notes _____

_____

_____

Name _____

Address _____

_____

Sample _____

Conversation Via _____

Sent _____ Follow Up _____

Enrolled _____ Stacked _____

Notes _____

_____

_____

Name _____

Address _____

_____

Sample _____

Conversation Via _____

Sent _____ Follow Up _____

Enrolled _____ Stacked _____

Notes _____

_____

_____

Sample Requests

Name _____

Address _____

_____

Sample _____

Conversation Via _____

Sent _____ Follow Up _____

Enrolled _____ Stacked _____

Notes _____

_____

_____

Name _____

Address _____

_____

Sample _____

Conversation Via _____

Sent _____ Follow Up _____

Enrolled _____ Stacked _____

Notes _____

_____

_____

Name _____

Address _____

_____

Sample _____

Conversation Via _____

Sent _____ Follow Up _____

Enrolled _____ Stacked _____

Notes _____

_____

_____

Name _____

Address _____

_____

Sample _____

Conversation Via _____

Sent _____ Follow Up _____

Enrolled _____ Stacked _____

Notes _____

_____

_____

Sample Requests

Name _____

Address _____

_____

Sample _____

Conversation Via _____

Sent _____ Follow Up _____

Enrolled _____ Stacked _____

Notes _____

_____

_____

Name _____

Address _____

_____

Sample _____

Conversation Via _____

Sent _____ Follow Up _____

Enrolled _____ Stacked _____

Notes _____

_____

_____

Name _____

Address _____

_____

Sample _____

Conversation Via _____

Sent _____ Follow Up _____

Enrolled _____ Stacked _____

Notes _____

_____

_____

Name _____

Address _____

_____

Sample _____

Conversation Via _____

Sent _____ Follow Up _____

Enrolled _____ Stacked _____

Notes _____

_____

_____

Sample Requests

Name _____

Address _____

_____

Sample _____

Conversation Via _____

Sent _____ Follow Up _____

Enrolled _____ Stacked _____

Notes _____

_____

_____

Name _____

Address _____

_____

Sample _____

Conversation Via _____

Sent _____ Follow Up _____

Enrolled _____ Stacked _____

Notes _____

_____

_____

Name _____

Address _____

_____

Sample _____

Conversation Via _____

Sent _____ Follow Up _____

Enrolled _____ Stacked _____

Notes _____

_____

_____

Name _____

Address _____

_____

Sample _____

Conversation Via _____

Sent _____ Follow Up _____

Enrolled _____ Stacked _____

Notes _____

_____

_____

Sample Requests

Name _____

Address _____

_____

Sample _____

Conversation Via _____

Sent _____ Follow Up _____

Enrolled _____ Stacked _____

Notes _____

_____

_____

Name _____

Address _____

_____

Sample _____

Conversation Via _____

Sent _____ Follow Up _____

Enrolled _____ Stacked _____

Notes _____

_____

_____

Name _____

Address _____

_____

Sample _____

Conversation Via _____

Sent _____ Follow Up _____

Enrolled _____ Stacked _____

Notes _____

_____

_____

Name _____

Address _____

_____

Sample _____

Conversation Via _____

Sent _____ Follow Up _____

Enrolled _____ Stacked _____

Notes _____

_____

_____

Sample Requests

Name _____

Address _____

_____

Sample _____

Conversation Via _____

Sent _____ Follow Up _____

Enrolled _____ Stacked _____

Notes _____

_____

_____

Name _____

Address _____

_____

Sample _____

Conversation Via _____

Sent _____ Follow Up _____

Enrolled _____ Stacked _____

Notes _____

_____

_____

Name _____

Address _____

_____

Sample _____

Conversation Via _____

Sent _____ Follow Up _____

Enrolled _____ Stacked _____

Notes _____

_____

_____

Name _____

Address _____

_____

Sample _____

Conversation Via _____

Sent _____ Follow Up _____

Enrolled _____ Stacked _____

Notes _____

_____

_____

Sample Requests

Name _____

Address _____

_____

Sample _____

Conversation Via _____

Sent _____ Follow Up _____

Enrolled _____ Stacked _____

Notes _____

_____

_____

Name _____

Address _____

_____

Sample _____

Conversation Via _____

Sent _____ Follow Up _____

Enrolled _____ Stacked _____

Notes _____

_____

_____

Name _____

Address _____

_____

Sample _____

Conversation Via _____

Sent _____ Follow Up _____

Enrolled _____ Stacked _____

Notes _____

_____

_____

Name _____

Address _____

_____

Sample _____

Conversation Via _____

Sent _____ Follow Up _____

Enrolled _____ Stacked _____

Notes _____

_____

_____

Sample Requests

Name _____

Address _____

_____

Sample _____

Conversation Via _____

Sent _____ Follow Up _____

Enrolled _____ Stacked _____

Notes _____

_____

_____

Name _____

Address _____

_____

Sample _____

Conversation Via _____

Sent _____ Follow Up _____

Enrolled _____ Stacked _____

Notes _____

_____

_____

Name _____

Address _____

_____

Sample _____

Conversation Via _____

Sent _____ Follow Up _____

Enrolled _____ Stacked _____

Notes _____

_____

_____

Name _____

Address _____

_____

Sample _____

Conversation Via _____

Sent _____ Follow Up _____

Enrolled _____ Stacked _____

Notes _____

_____

_____

Sample Requests

Name _____

Address _____

_____

Sample _____

Conversation Via _____

Sent _____ Follow Up _____

Enrolled _____ Stacked _____

Notes _____

_____

_____

Name _____

Address _____

_____

Sample _____

Conversation Via _____

Sent _____ Follow Up _____

Enrolled _____ Stacked _____

Notes _____

_____

_____

Name _____

Address _____

_____

Sample _____

Conversation Via _____

Sent _____ Follow Up _____

Enrolled _____ Stacked _____

Notes _____

_____

_____

Name _____

Address _____

_____

Sample _____

Conversation Via _____

Sent _____ Follow Up _____

Enrolled _____ Stacked _____

Notes _____

_____

_____

Sample Requests

Name _____

Address _____

_____

Sample _____

Conversation Via _____

Sent _____ Follow Up _____

Enrolled _____ Stacked _____

Notes _____

_____

_____

Name _____

Address _____

_____

Sample _____

Conversation Via _____

Sent _____ Follow Up _____

Enrolled _____ Stacked _____

Notes _____

_____

_____

Name _____

Address _____

_____

Sample _____

Conversation Via _____

Sent _____ Follow Up _____

Enrolled _____ Stacked _____

Notes _____

_____

_____

Name _____

Address _____

_____

Sample _____

Conversation Via _____

Sent _____ Follow Up _____

Enrolled _____ Stacked _____

Notes _____

_____

_____

Sample Requests

Name _____

Address _____

_____

Sample _____

Conversation Via _____

Sent _____ Follow Up _____

Enrolled _____ Stacked _____

Notes _____

_____

_____

Name _____

Address _____

_____

Sample _____

Conversation Via _____

Sent _____ Follow Up _____

Enrolled _____ Stacked _____

Notes _____

_____

_____

Name _____

Address _____

_____

Sample _____

Conversation Via _____

Sent _____ Follow Up _____

Enrolled _____ Stacked _____

Notes _____

_____

_____

Name _____

Address _____

_____

Sample _____

Conversation Via _____

Sent _____ Follow Up _____

Enrolled _____ Stacked _____

Notes _____

_____

_____

Sample Requests

Name _____

Address _____

_____

Sample _____

Conversation Via _____

Sent _____ Follow Up _____

Enrolled _____ Stacked _____

Notes _____

_____

_____

Name _____

Address _____

_____

Sample _____

Conversation Via _____

Sent _____ Follow Up _____

Enrolled _____ Stacked _____

Notes _____

_____

_____

Name _____

Address _____

_____

Sample _____

Conversation Via _____

Sent _____ Follow Up _____

Enrolled _____ Stacked _____

Notes _____

_____

_____

Name _____

Address _____

_____

Sample _____

Conversation Via _____

Sent _____ Follow Up _____

Enrolled _____ Stacked _____

Notes _____

_____

_____

Sample Requests

Name _____

Address _____

_____

Sample _____

Conversation Via _____

Sent _____ Follow Up _____

Enrolled _____ Stacked _____

Notes _____

_____

_____

Name _____

Address _____

_____

Sample _____

Conversation Via _____

Sent _____ Follow Up _____

Enrolled _____ Stacked _____

Notes _____

_____

_____

Name _____

Address _____

_____

Sample _____

Conversation Via _____

Sent _____ Follow Up _____

Enrolled _____ Stacked _____

Notes _____

_____

_____

Name _____

Address _____

_____

Sample _____

Conversation Via _____

Sent _____ Follow Up _____

Enrolled _____ Stacked _____

Notes _____

_____

_____

Sample Requests

Name _____

Address _____

_____

Sample _____

Conversation Via _____

Sent _____ Follow Up _____

Enrolled _____ Stacked _____

Notes _____

_____

_____

Name _____

Address _____

_____

Sample _____

Conversation Via _____

Sent _____ Follow Up _____

Enrolled _____ Stacked _____

Notes _____

_____

_____

Name _____

Address _____

_____

Sample _____

Conversation Via _____

Sent _____ Follow Up _____

Enrolled _____ Stacked _____

Notes _____

_____

_____

Name _____

Address _____

_____

Sample _____

Conversation Via _____

Sent _____ Follow Up _____

Enrolled _____ Stacked _____

Notes _____

_____

_____

Sample Requests

Name _____

Address _____

_____

Sample _____

Conversation Via _____

Sent _____ Follow Up _____

Enrolled _____ Stacked _____

Notes _____

_____

_____

Name _____

Address _____

_____

Sample _____

Conversation Via _____

Sent _____ Follow Up _____

Enrolled _____ Stacked _____

Notes _____

_____

_____

Name _____

Address _____

_____

Sample _____

Conversation Via _____

Sent _____ Follow Up _____

Enrolled _____ Stacked _____

Notes _____

_____

_____

Name _____

Address _____

_____

Sample _____

Conversation Via _____

Sent _____ Follow Up _____

Enrolled _____ Stacked _____

Notes _____

_____

_____

Sample Requests

Name _____

Address _____

_____

Sample _____

Conversation Via _____

Sent _____ Follow Up _____

Enrolled _____ Stacked _____

Notes _____

_____

_____

Name _____

Address _____

_____

Sample _____

Conversation Via _____

Sent _____ Follow Up _____

Enrolled _____ Stacked _____

Notes _____

_____

_____

Name _____

Address _____

_____

Sample _____

Conversation Via _____

Sent _____ Follow Up _____

Enrolled _____ Stacked _____

Notes _____

_____

_____

Name _____

Address _____

_____

Sample _____

Conversation Via _____

Sent _____ Follow Up _____

Enrolled _____ Stacked _____

Notes _____

_____

_____

Sample Requests

Name _____

Address _____

_____

Sample _____

Conversation Via _____

Sent _____ Follow Up _____

Enrolled _____ Stacked _____

Notes _____

_____

_____

Name _____

Address _____

_____

Sample _____

Conversation Via _____

Sent _____ Follow Up _____

Enrolled _____ Stacked _____

Notes _____

_____

_____

Name _____

Address _____

_____

Sample _____

Conversation Via _____

Sent _____ Follow Up _____

Enrolled _____ Stacked _____

Notes _____

_____

_____

Name _____

Address _____

_____

Sample _____

Conversation Via _____

Sent _____ Follow Up _____

Enrolled _____ Stacked _____

Notes _____

_____

_____

Sample Requests

Name _____

Address _____

_____

Sample _____

Conversation Via _____

Sent _____ Follow Up _____

Enrolled _____ Stacked _____

Notes _____

_____

_____

Name _____

Address _____

_____

Sample _____

Conversation Via _____

Sent _____ Follow Up _____

Enrolled _____ Stacked _____

Notes _____

_____

_____

Name _____

Address _____

_____

Sample _____

Conversation Via _____

Sent _____ Follow Up _____

Enrolled _____ Stacked _____

Notes _____

_____

_____

Name _____

Address _____

_____

Sample _____

Conversation Via _____

Sent _____ Follow Up _____

Enrolled _____ Stacked _____

Notes _____

_____

_____

Sample Requests

Name _____

Address _____

_____

Sample _____

Conversation Via _____

Sent _____ Follow Up _____

Enrolled _____ Stacked _____

Notes _____

_____

_____

Name _____

Address _____

_____

Sample _____

Conversation Via _____

Sent _____ Follow Up _____

Enrolled _____ Stacked _____

Notes _____

_____

_____

Name _____

Address _____

_____

Sample _____

Conversation Via _____

Sent _____ Follow Up _____

Enrolled _____ Stacked _____

Notes _____

_____

_____

Name _____

Address _____

_____

Sample _____

Conversation Via _____

Sent _____ Follow Up _____

Enrolled _____ Stacked _____

Notes _____

_____

_____

Sample Requests

Name _____

Address _____

_____

Sample _____

Conversation Via _____

Sent _____ Follow Up _____

Enrolled _____ Stacked _____

Notes _____

_____

_____

Name _____

Address _____

_____

Sample _____

Conversation Via _____

Sent _____ Follow Up _____

Enrolled _____ Stacked _____

Notes _____

_____

_____

Name _____

Address _____

_____

Sample _____

Conversation Via _____

Sent _____ Follow Up _____

Enrolled _____ Stacked _____

Notes _____

_____

_____

Name _____

Address _____

_____

Sample _____

Conversation Via _____

Sent _____ Follow Up _____

Enrolled _____ Stacked _____

Notes _____

_____

_____

Ideas & Doodles

Ideas & Doodles

Ideas & Doodles

Ideas & Doodles

Ideas & Doodles

Ideas & Doodles

Ideas & Doodles

Ideas & Doodles

Made in the USA
Middletown, DE
26 November 2017